Caterpillar to Butterfly

Melvin and Gilda Berger

SCHOLASTIC INC.

New York Toronto London Auckland Sydney
Mexico City New Delhi Hong Kong Buenos Aires

Photographs: Cover: Dwight Kuhn; p. 1: Robert & Linda Mitchell; p. 3: Dwight Kuhn; p. 4: Greg Dimijian/Photo Researchers, Inc.; p. 5: Robert & Linda Mitchell; p. 6: Dwight Kuhn; p. 7: John Marechal/Bruce Coleman Inc.; p. 8: Robert & Linda Mitchell; p. 9: Harry Rogers/Photo Researchers, Inc.; p. 10: Robert & Linda Mitchell; p. 11: Robert & Linda Mitchell; p. 12: Robert & Linda Mitchell; p. 13: Robert & Linda Mitchell; p. 14: Robert & Linda Mitchell; p. 15: Stephen Dalton/Photo Researchers, Inc.; p. 16: M. Fogden/Bruce Coleman Inc.

Photo Research: Sarah Longacre

ISBN 0-439-57483-8

12 11 10 9 8 7 6 5 4 3 2   4 5 6 7 8 9/0
                                                      08

Printed in the U.S.A.
First printing, March 2004

A butterfly is an insect.

The mother butterfly lays eggs.

Most butterfly eggs are green or yellow.

A caterpillar grows
inside each egg.

Fun Fact

After it hatches, the caterpillar eats its shell.

The caterpillar comes out of the egg.

Fun Fact
The first leaf that the caterpillar eats is the leaf on which it was born.

The caterpillar eats leaves.

The caterpillar grows and grows.

Fun Fact

To grow, the caterpillar sheds its old skin and gets a new, bigger one.

The caterpillar gets very big.

The big caterpillar hangs
down from a branch.

The caterpillar makes a hard shell.
It is called a pupa.

The pupa changes
into a butterfly.

The butterfly comes out of the shell.

The butterfly flies away.

The new butterfly lays eggs
on a leaf.